Straight from the Heart and Other Stories

Straight from the Heart and Other Stories

Lisa Calderone-Stewart
Ed Kunzman

Saint Mary's Press
Christian Brothers Publications
Winona, Minnesota

We dedicate this book to the next generation:

Emily Jean Banset
Rebecca Ann Banset
Thomas Joseph Banset
Nicholas Robert Bidroski
Scott Jeffrey Bidroski
Andrea Elaine Bottger
Kristin Marie Bottger
Sean Norman Bottger
Barbara Ann Calderone
Bernadette Rose Calderone
Elizabeth Constance Calderone
Elizabeth Katherine Grubb
Sarah Irene Grubb
Eric Michael Hagan
Kelly Suzanne Hagan
Mary Elizabeth Hagan
Christine Michelle Hladik
Gregory Stewart Hladik
Jennifer Susan Hladik
Robert Joseph Hladik
Adam Franklin Jacobs
Billie Lee Kunzman

Paige Denise Kunzman
Rahne Lane Kunzman
Ri Albert Kunzman
Conor Patrick McGhehey
Jill Renee McGhehey
Molly Maureen McGhehey
Tate David McGhehey
Casey (KC) John Moscrip
Hilary Ann Moscrip
Jared Paul Moscrip
Brian James Stewart
Jill Elizabeth Stewart
Kelsey Lynn Stewart
Kerry Jean Stewart
Michael James Stewart
Ralph Pierre Stewart
Brianna Lynn Thompson
David Edward Towey
Elizabeth Susan Towey
Aaron Thomas Willey
Gretchen Michelle Willey
Richard Paul Willey

The precious gift of faith that we were given we now happily hand on to you—in fulfillment of Jesus' desire: "The gift you have received, give as a gift" (Matthew 10:8).

Genuine recycled paper with 10% post-consumer waste.
Printed with soy-based ink.

The publishing team included Brian Singer-Towns, development editor; Cheryl Drivdahl, copy editor; Alan S. Hanson, production editor and typesetter; Stephan Nagel, cover designer; Click Art, T/Maker Company, cover image; pre-press, printing, and binding by the graphics division of Saint Mary's Press.

The acknowledgments continue on page 70.

Printed in the United States of America

Printing: 9 8 7 6 5 4 3 2 1

Year: 2007 06 05 04 03 02 01 00 99

ISBN 0-88489-592-0

Contents

Preface

Life is filled with opportunities for sharing stories. We share stories with classmates at school, with friends at parties, and with relatives at family gatherings. We read stories in books, watch stories on television and in movies, and write stories for English class. We even read stories in chat rooms on the Internet and swap stories by e-mail.

Whenever we listen to good stories, we find ourselves responding in a variety of ways: we laugh and we cry, we tremble in fear and we sigh in relief, we shake our head in disbelief and we nod in agreement. We respond in these ways because good stories are like mirrors: they give us a reflection of ourselves. The joys and sorrows of the stories' characters reflect our own joys and sorrows: we laugh and we cry from the heart because we recognize ourselves in the tales being told.

Some of the most meaningful stories that people share focus on growing up. These are stories of going to school and playing sports, of losing friends and finding new ones, of falling in love and breaking up. These are also stories that try to deal with the big questions of life: What kind of person do I want to be?

Where is my life going? How do I relate to my family? What kinds of people do I want for friends? How do I make difficult decisions? What do I really believe in? Who is God?

This book is a collection of stories about young people. The characters in these stories experience wonder and struggle, hurt and forgiveness, failure and success, tears and laughter, learning and relearning. In other words, these stories are very much like your own. You are invited to use them as mirrors for looking at your own life.

After every story in this book, you will find a set of questions to help you take a deeper look at yourself. The title of this set of questions is "Seeing Your Own Story." When you think about the issues and events in your own life that the stories reflect back to you, you can begin to see yourself in a new light and learn more about the unique person you are.

After the reflection questions is a section called "Seeing the Faith Story." This section is designed to help you make connections between what you are discovering about yourself and what it means to be a believer in God, a Christian, and a Catholic. The questions at the end of this section can help you view your own life through the eyes of faith.

This book is one in a series of five. The other books in the series are entitled *That First Kiss and Other Stories, My Wish List and Other Stories, Better than Natural and Other*

Stories, and *Meeting Frankenstein and Other Stories.* Each book in the series presents several opportunities for you to discover more about your own story, to examine your own issues, and to search for your own answers about life, God, and faith.

It is our hope that once you see your deeper self through the mirrors of these stories, you will continue to reflect on the important matters of life. We believe that life becomes happier and more meaningful when we take the time to be reflective. A word of caution: Looking into the mirror of a story may become an exciting, lifelong habit!

Straight from the Heart

Dear Gabby,

I am a seventeen-year-old who works at a fast-food restaurant on weekends. Last Saturday when I was grilling hamburgers with three other guys, one of them remarked how pretty his girlfriend was. A second one—let's call him Hank—said: "Well, nothing's as pretty as 'Hilary' over there when she bends over. I can't wait for her to drop another dollar."

Because Hank has a big mouth, most of the employees heard what he said, including Hilary, who turned around from the cash register and blushed. Her face turned redder when the four of us began to laugh. Later that night, we were called to the manager's office and told that we had to refrain from making further sexual comments. "There are laws against sexual harassment, guys," the manager told us, "and whether you like it or not, you've got to obey them if you want a job here. Besides, Hilary was crying when she told me what happened. I don't think she should have to come to work and worry about being offended by your crass remarks."

I can't believe there are laws against having fun at work! Hank didn't pinch Hilary or try to kiss her or call her a foul name. He just complimented her on her good looks. If I were Hilary, I would be flattered. Instead, she cried and made a big issue of a harmless joke. What don't I understand? Have I missed out on something? Was I dozing in class when the teacher told us that girls don't like to be complimented anymore?

Sleeping in Seattle

» » » « « «

Dear Sleeping,

There's a world of difference between a genuine compliment and sexual harassment. First off, compliments are offered not in jest, but very openly and honestly. Second, compliments make one feel not smaller, but bigger, because unlike sexual harassment, they do not reduce a person to a bodily function or part, but respect the whole person. Third, true compliments come straight from the heart, not from the groin. Yes, women still enjoy sincere compliments, but few of us enjoy being harassed.

Why are there laws against sexual harassment? For the same reason that there are laws against speeding and stealing: because people would get hurt if there weren't. If we lived in a perfect world, we would not need any laws because everyone would always choose what is good and avoid what is bad. However, the world is far from perfect, and therefore, laws are necessary. How many people would drive sixty miles per hour on city streets if there were no speed limit? How many people would take things that didn't belong to them if stealing were not illegal? How many people would let their sexual energy run wild at work or at school if there were no laws against sexual harassment? You see, we need laws both to protect us and to guide us.

I realize that this response is already too long, but I want to tell you a short story before I conclude. One day, two men were walking to their cars after work when one of them pointed across the street and cried: "Wow! What a beautiful babe!" The other man looked to where his coworker was pointing and said: "Oh, really? I don't even know her, Steve." "Are you blind?" Steve asked in disbelief. "Just look at that face, Joe!" "Oh, I can see her face all right," Joe responded, "but I can't see her heart." "What?" Steve exclaimed, hardly believing his ears. "Well, you see," Joe tried to explain, "the girl I took to my senior prom was considered the plainest Jane in the class, but I fell in love with her and married her. She's beautiful, Steve, all the way to the bottom of her heart."

When you finally wake up in Seattle, try to learn a lesson from Joe about respect for others. Until you and your coworkers learn that lesson, I, for one, will be glad that there are laws against sexual harassment.

Gabby

Seeing Your Own Story

- Did Hilary overreact to Hank's remark and his friends' laughter? In your opinion, was she really the victim of sexual harassment?
- Think of two commandments or laws that young people have difficulty understanding. What are the values that these commandments or laws try to safeguard? Why are these values important?

Seeing the Faith Story

Of the many lists of laws in the Bible, the Ten Commandments—"You shall not make wrongful use of the name of the LORD your God," "Honor your father and your mother," "You shall not murder," and the rest (Exodus 20:2–17)—are the most famous. These Commandments point to certain clear values and insist on their importance in human life: for example, love of God, respect for parents, and respect for the lives of others.

Unlike the virtues, which guide a person from *the inside,* the Commandments guide a person from *the outside.* Because there is sin

15

in the world, because people are at different stages of moral development, and because people don't always understand what is truly good, the commandments and laws are necessary to preserve order and peace in the human community. In this story, Gabby insisted on the importance of laws both as protectors of people and as guideposts for making good decisions.

The stories in this book focus on the Ten Commandments and what they teach us about ourselves in our relationships with God and one another. By familiarizing ourselves with the Commandments, we come to recognize the values they highlight, and we learn to choose those values every day—not because we have to, but because we want to.

- Think about a situation in which you chose to do the right thing only because you knew that you would get into trouble if you didn't. Now think about a situation in which you chose to do the right thing because you knew it was the right thing to do.

Moses . . . said . . . : Hear, O Israel, the statutes and ordinances that I am addressing to you today. (Deuteronomy 5:1)

Taking a Cookie Break

As Jason Izquierdo walked home from school, he was on the verge of tears. For the past month, he had been campaigning tirelessly for the office of student council president— not because he really wanted to be president, but because his father wanted him to be president. "You're a poor athlete, son, and a lousy student," Mr. Izquierdo had pressured him. "You don't want to be a loser all your life, do you? When I was your age, I was the first-string quarterback and starting center on the basketball team and . . ." After hearing for the thousandth time the catalog of his father's athletic feats in high school, Jason had finally proposed running for student council secretary. "Secretary? That's a girl's job!" his father had answered. "Run for president. You're an Izquierdo! You deserve the best! Do something with your life, son!"

What did Jason really want to do with his life? He wanted to practice the piano, write music, sing in a big choir, and study to be a music teacher. When he was involved with his music, the hours passed like minutes, and the constant criticism by his father was forgotten.

It was as if he were in communication with Something bigger, Something beyond himself.

Since agreeing to run for the student council, Jason hadn't found much time for his music. That very morning at school, his music teacher had kept him after class to ask him why he hadn't learned the new songs for the spring recital. "You promised to accompany the swing choir, Jason, but you hardly know the pieces," Ms. Langan had scolded him. "Do I need to look for someone else? Let me know tomorrow."

Jason shook his head in desperation as he walked down the sidewalk. His dad would never let him live it down if he lost the student council race, yet he didn't want to disappoint his music teacher, either. The timing of Ms. Langan's warning couldn't have been worse—just as he was hearing from others that he was running the best campaign and would probably be elected. What a mess! He didn't have time for what he really loved to do (make music) because all his free time was spent doing something he really didn't care about (getting elected to the student council). If only he didn't have to prove himself to his father! If only!

Ms. Langan probably won't ask me to be next year's accompanist, he said to himself sadly, kicking a pebble down the sidewalk. And Jake's going to find another best friend soon; every time he's called, I've been too busy to go out. And worst of all, I don't even sit down at the piano anymore before I go to bed. That's how I always used to end the day.

Jason was lost in these thoughts as he passed by his grandmother's house. When she called to him from her flower garden, he jumped a foot off the cement. "Jason, come have a cookie with your granny."

"Sorry, I'm too busy, Gran," he said, his heart pounding from the surprise. "I've got to get home."

"Nonsense," she laughed, waving off his concerns with her hoe. "Life's never too busy for a cookie break. Come talk to your granny."

Jason shook his head and smiled at the gray-haired woman, crossed the grass to her garden, and walked with her into the house. It took her only five minutes to get the whole story out of him. She sipped coffee and listened attentively as her grandson ate a peanut butter cookie and unburdened his heavy heart.

"You know, Jason," she said when he had finished talking, "you've got a tough nut to crack there. But I think I can make it easier."

"How?" He was curious to hear his grandmother's words of wisdom. "Dad, Ms. Langan, and Jake are all after me. I can't win this one, Gran, I just can't win."

Offering him another cookie, she winked slyly and sat back in her chair. "It's not a question of winning or losing, Jason, or of making anybody else happy. It's a matter of knowing what's most important in life."

He wrinkled his nose as he bit into the second cookie. "Like what?"

"Like praying more often," she replied without pausing to think.

"I don't have time to pray," he smirked, "and I don't like praying anyway."

"You don't?" She seemed truly surprised. "You just told me that when you used to play the piano at the end of the day, it was like connecting with Something bigger than yourself. Couldn't that Something bigger be God? Why not give that Something bigger a little space each day by playing the piano before you go to bed, and the other things will sort themselves out eventually."

"But Dad thinks musicians are losers," Jason said, unconvinced.

"Only musicians who don't make music are losers," his grandmother answered with a wink. "And children of God who don't pray."

"Well, how do you pray, Gran?" Jason asked, still doubting.

"What do you think I was doing on my knees out there in the garden?" she laughed. "It's not just the tulips I talk to, you know!"

Seeing Your Own Story

- If you could speak for Jason, what would you say to Mr. Izquierdo? Is excelling in athletics or academics more important than excelling in music?

Seeing the Faith Story

The first commandment urges us to put God first in life. Nothing else deserves the kind of devotion and love that we owe to God alone. Nevertheless, many people and causes and things demand our time and energy, and we are often tempted to place them ahead of God, to make false gods of them. The Bible calls these false gods idols, and worshiping them idolatry.

Jason struggled to sort out many conflicting demands in his life and didn't know what to do. His grandmother reminded him that there is only one way to find true balance and purpose in life: to put God in first place every day.

- When you feel the pressure of many commitments and deadlines, how do you decide what to do first? Where does God fit in your busy schedule?
- Some claim that few U.S. citizens pray or go to church anymore, that people in the United States today lack religious values and respect for God. Do you agree or disagree? Why?

I am the LORD your God . . . ; you shall have no other gods before me. (Exodus 20:2–3)

Ice Cream, TV, and Baby-Sitting

Eric was baby-sitting for the first time. Originally, the idea of this job hadn't exactly turned him on—after all, what kind of fun could it be to stay home with a six-year-old all day Saturday? But when he had discovered he could make five dollars an hour, suddenly he had become quite interested.

Eric was the youngest of the family, so he had no little brothers or sisters. He didn't really know a lot about six-year-olds, but he had seen them at family parties from time to time. He had some younger cousins—and hadn't each of them been six at some point? So he figured he'd be able to handle the challenge.

No problem, thought Eric. Stay home alone, watch TV, talk on the phone; feed the kid some cereal in the morning and a peanut butter sandwich at noon, maybe a snack later; give him some toys to play with; and collect forty dollars. I can make this work.

When it was time for lunch, little Tommy walked out of the TV room, and into the hallway where Eric was talking to one of his friends on the phone. "I want a Goddammit ice cream," he announced.

"TOMMY!" Eric shouted at him, and then said, "Call you back later!" into the phone as he slammed down the receiver and grabbed the child. "Don't talk like that!"

"Let go of me, Goddammit!" Tommy commanded.

Eric couldn't believe his ears. "Where did you hear words like that?"

Tommy just repeated his first request. "Eric, I want a Goddammit ice cream."

Eric was sure that Tommy's parents never used language like that. He couldn't imagine who had taught Tommy this new word. He tried again to get Tommy's attention. "Tommy, listen to me. Look at me. It's not nice to say 'God-anything' unless you are saying something in a special way, like in a prayer. Don't go around saying God's name unless you are really talking about God. And don't say 'damn' at all. That's a bad word. Do you understand me, Tommy?"

Tommy nodded. "Can I have an ice cream?"

"Sure, let's eat some together," Eric answered.

They went into the kitchen, and Eric opened the freezer and got out the carton of ice cream. He turned around, and Tommy was gone. Then Eric heard raw language and gunshots coming from the TV room. He wondered whether Tommy had been watching R-rated movies and music videos all morning. Eric dashed into the TV room, clicked off the TV, took Tommy's hand, and led him back into the kitchen. "Let's have our ice cream in here, and later we can read some books, okay?" Eric was beginning to realize that there was more to baby-sitting than he had originally thought.

As they ate their ice cream together, Eric began to remember all the times his mother had not let him buy certain CDs and tapes because of their "language." He had thought it was stupid until now. He had thought his mother was just paranoid. But now Eric observed how easily a six-year-old could pick up bad language and make it his own after just a few hours of watching TV.

Tommy, the six-year-old, had just taught Eric a lesson his mother had been trying to teach him for years.

Seeing Your Own Story

- If Eric had been playing with Tommy and supervising him better, Tommy wouldn't have watched programs with foul language all morning. Do you think Eric was responsible for Tommy's learning his new word, even though Eric didn't directly teach him that word? What will Tommy's parents think if the little boy tries his new word out on them?
- Do you think the language on TV, on the radio, and in movies has gotten out of hand? Why or why not?

Seeing the Faith Story

Giving respect to God's name is a very old tradition. The world's major religions all hold that God's name is precious and sacred. In fact, the Jews, God's Chosen People, were taught never even to say God's name out loud. Yet today, "Goddammit" doesn't even shock most teenagers. We can hear profanity on the radio, on most TV channels, and in most movies. Sometimes, we don't even notice how bad it has become until we hear a young child use offensive language.

- How about your own language? If someone recorded all the language you use in a typical day, and played the tape back for a parent or grandparent to hear, would you be embarrassed or proud? How are respecting God and using respectful language related?

You shall not make wrongful use of the name of the LORD your God. (Exodus 20:7)

The Guy in the Tie

Every Sunday morning, Nathan had the same
fight with his parents. "I don't want to go to
Mass! I hate church! I don't see why I should
have to go. It does nothing for me. It's a waste
of time!"

Every Sunday morning, Nathan still had to
go. This Sunday was no exception. He wanted
to wear jeans. They said no. His jeans were
too worn-out—not "crisp" enough for church.
What does *crisp* mean? Who wears crisp jeans?
Crisp is what you want your cracker to be.
Crisp has nothing to do with jeans.

He wanted to wear his new T-shirt. "It's new
and *crisp!*" he tried to argue. No, they said. His
new T-shirt had all those words on it, and people would be too distracted. They'd be reading
his T-shirt instead of praying. I wish someone
would wear a T-shirt like this and stand in
front of me, he thought. It would give me
something to do—ease the boredom a bit.

He didn't even bother asking them whether
he could wear his running shoes.

So once again, Nathan had to go to church
in his *crisp* cotton pants, his *nice* shirt, and
his *decent* shoes. He felt stupid and embar-

rassed and begged his parents not to make him sit in the front row of the church. But they did anyway.

He looked around, trying to see what other parents had made their kids wear. Some kids were in jeans, although several of them were actually wearing newer looking jeans. (When he got a new pair of jeans, maybe he'd ask if they were crisp enough for church!) Many were in nice shirts. But many were in T-shirts (some with a lot of words!), and some were in old running shoes as well. Then he spied a guy in a tie! Wow, his parents must have had some argument with him! Nathan was glad his parents didn't make him wear a tie.

Nathan heard some noise and turned around. He saw a few families that had just come in together; they had teenage sons and daughters who were greeting one another and laughing. The families were sitting together. Some of those teenagers were dressed in jeans and T-shirts, but some of them were wearing nicer stuff. One of the girls was even wearing a dress! She looked really good.

As he turned back around, Nathan searched for the guy with the tie. What had happened to him? Nathan couldn't find him anywhere. He thought perhaps the guy had decided to sneak off someplace and remove his tie before his parents noticed.

When Mass began, Nathan saw the guy with the tie again. Now he realized why the guy was so dressed up. He was walking in with the big book! Wow, he looked important. He looked as if he knew what he was doing.

He did know what he was doing. He was good. He was prepared. When he proclaimed the first reading, Nathan heard and understood every word. Nathan seldom paid attention when an adult read.

Nathan must have daydreamed through the second reading. The next thing he knew, everyone was singing, "Alleluia," and standing for the Gospel. He heard the voices from that group of families with the teenagers. They were actually singing out loud. Nathan almost never sang. He wondered what they were so pumped up about. He noticed that the guy in the tie was now sitting with that group of families. That girl in the dress really looked nice.

Nathan fumbled through the pages of the songbook, hunting for the verse they were singing. He wasn't planning to sing himself, but he thought maybe he would look at the words so that he could follow along.

Seeing Your Own Story

- Why did Nathan decide to look through the songbook and find the Alleluia verse that was being sung? What made him choose to get a bit more involved?
- The girl in the dress and the other friends of the guy with the tie were paying atten-

tion to the Mass, perhaps more than usual because one of their friends had an important part to play. How would a feeling of being connected with what's happening at Mass affect a person's attitude about Mass?

Seeing the Faith Story

The Sunday liturgy, also called Mass by Catholics, is a community celebration of prayer. God asks us to keep one day of the week holy, and to honor that sacred time and sacred space. For many young people, like Nathan, it's difficult to feel excited about going to church. Sometimes, adults feel the same way. Perhaps they wish Mass could be more entertaining. But our role as a community gathered to pray is not to sit back and let things happen so that we can watch and be entertained. Our role is to be an active part of the worship. When we are actively involved in something, we understand it more, and it becomes less boring to us.

- How would the pace of life be affected if everyone actually observed one day a week as a holy day of rest from everyday pressures and stress? How might this habit make life better for you and others? Would you be willing to participate in such a practice?
- How do you feel about going to Mass on Sunday or on Saturday evening? Do you feel

the same as Nathan did? If so, how can you improve your attitude about going to Mass? If you already have a positive attitude, what has helped you develop it when so many other teens have not?

Remember the sabbath day, and keep it holy. (Exodus 20:8)

A Real Man

Matt Leahy and two of his classmates were in the basement watching the Green Bay Packers and the Chicago Bears on the big-screen TV. It was halftime, and Matt had just returned from a snack run upstairs. After giving each of his friends a can of Pepsi and opening a new bag of chips, he fell into the deep cushions of the couch and groaned. Gabe looked at him with a question mark in his eyes.

"What are you moaning about? Your team's winning, right?"

"Yeah, the Packers are ahead," he answered, "but I'm still losing the war with Mom. I talked to her again when I was upstairs, but she hasn't changed her mind: I still can't go to Jack's party on Saturday."

"Why not?" Tyler asked, popping the top of the aluminum can and reaching for the potato chips.

"Because Jack's older brother's an alcoholic, and she wants to keep me away from bad influences." Matt shook his head and hit the pillow in his lap. "Besides, his parents'll be out of town."

"Yeah, but Jack's as clean as they come," Gabe laughed. "I've never even seen him sniff a beer."

"I've told Mom a hundred times that I'm only going to play football and watch the college games on TV, but she won't give in," Matt explained. "She's convinced that Jack's brother's going to bring a keg, and I'll be pressured to drink."

"Then what are you going to do?" Gabe asked impatiently.

"I don't know," Matt sighed. "Probably sit here and mope all day Saturday."

The air was heavy with Matt's frustration as the three listened to the TV announcer excitedly recapping the first-half statistics. When another commercial started, Tyler grabbed a handful of potato chips and turned to his host.

"Matt," he said, "my dad beat me with a belt when I came home drunk after homecoming last year. You're not the only one who has strict parents. Gosh, I haven't had a swig of beer since last October."

"You guys don't have any backbone," Gabe sneered with a toss of his head. "Listen to the two of you: 'I can't go to Jack's because Mommy's afraid I'll get drunk.' 'I can't drink because Daddy's going to beat the devil out of me.' Will you still be calling Mommy and Daddy for permission when you're in college?"

As the second half began with a powerful kick into the end zone, Matt sat up and spoke without taking his eyes off the TV. "There's a big difference between having no backbone, Gabe, and listening to your parents. I don't think I'm a weakling because I listen to my mom. She loves me and doesn't want me to get hurt, that's all."

"And I suppose Tyler's dad loves him, too, and hits him with a belt to prove it," Gabe snorted. "We're juniors in high school, guys. Why can't parents and teachers treat us like grownups instead of babies?"

Another long silence fell upon the three friends. Although they seemed to be watching the game with rapt attention, their minds were far from Soldier Field in Chicago, where the Packers were drubbing the Bears. The third quarter was almost over before Tyler smashed his empty Pepsi can between his hands and tossed it into the trash can by the wall.

"Gabe," he said, "I think you owe Matt an apology. Mrs. Leahy's a great mother, and you know it. I wish my dad would talk to me instead of using a belt to make his point."

"I just wish all parents would drop off the face of the earth," Gabe replied. "Then we could make our own decisions and do whatever we wanted."

"I don't think it's that easy, Gabe," Matt said carefully. "There will always be people we have to listen to and take advice from. Don't you think the Bears and Packers have to listen to their coaches? Don't the teachers at school have to answer to the principal? I guess you're right to be upset about Tyler's getting hit with a belt, but that doesn't mean that parents have no use in the world. My mom has done more for me than I'll ever know."

"Why am I sitting here and listening to this lecture?" Gabe cried, standing up and moving to the stairs. "I'm going to Jack's to watch the game with a *real man.*"

As his footsteps sounded loudly on the stairs, Matt turned to Tyler and smiled weakly. "Are you going to Jack's next Saturday?" he asked his hungry friend, who was now finishing off the last crumbs in the bag of chips.

"I was," Tyler said between bites, "but not now. How about coming over to my house instead?"

Seeing Your Own Story

- Do you think Matt's mother was overprotective? Was Tyler being disrespectful of his father by telling Matt and Gabe that he had been beaten with a belt? Was that a "family secret" that should have been kept secret? If you had been there, what would you have said to Tyler?

Seeing the Faith Story

Christians believe that respect for parents is something that God asks of us, no matter how old we are. As children and adolescents, we honor our parents by seeking and heeding their advice; as adults, we honor our parents by seeing to their needs while they grow older. At all ages, we honor our parents by loving them and praying for their welfare.

God intends for parents to love their children and for families to be safe havens. Unfortunately, for some young people, this situation does not exist. Children are never obligated to obey their parents when doing so would result in harm to themselves or others, or to submit willingly to any kind of assault from members of their family. We need to use our God-given intelligence to distinguish good advice from bad advice and to remove ourselves from abusive situations.

- How do you show respect for your parents on a daily basis? When you find it difficult to obey one of their orders, do you try to discuss its reasonableness with them, or do you keep your feelings to yourself? In your opinion, is it more difficult for parents to let their children do whatever they like or to set limits for their children? Why?
- Describe a situation in which a teenager would be wrong to disobey his parents. Describe a situation in which a teenager would be right to disobey her parents. What makes the two situations different?

Honor your father and your mother. (Exodus 20:12)

It's Wrong No Matter Who Does It

"That good-for-nothing finally got what he deserved!" Mr. Racjik said with a thump of his fist on the breakfast table. "I wish they'd asked me to give the lethal injection—I'd have broken his stupid neck first." He noisily refolded the morning paper and tossed it into an empty chair.

"So, one killing justifies another?" Mrs. Racjik challenged him. She was standing by the coffeemaker, waiting for the last drops to fall through the filter. "Do you know that the poor boy grew up in the slums of New York? He was beaten senseless whenever his mother's boyfriend got drunk—and even lost an eye when his cousin shot him during an argument."

"So, you're defending the murderer because he had a tough childhood?" Mr. Racjik said, the red rising in his cheeks. "What about the fact that he raped and murdered those cheerleaders? Do we just slap his hand because he couldn't control himself?"

"What he did was wrong, I agree," Mrs. Racjik explained calmly, pouring herself a cup of coffee and sitting across from her husband. "But his execution hardly brings those girls back from the dead, does it? Now, there's just more blood spilt, and no one's better off! You're just like that crazy preacher in Florida who shot the doctor at the abortion clinic. By some twist of logic, he felt justified in killing the doctor to save the unborn."

"At least he was defending innocent babies," Mr. Racjik cried defensively. "That's why I vote for Republicans: they care about the unborn. You always vote for proabortion Democrats!"

"Well, there's more to politics than abortion!" Mrs. Racjik replied, beginning to lose her composure. She blew the steam from her coffee and sipped the hot liquid carefully before speaking again. "Anyway, I can understand why certain women seek an abortion. Beth Horner, my best friend in high school, had one because she was only fifteen and her father threatened to kick her out of the house. And Samantha Sherwood terminated her last pregnancy because the fetus was deformed."

Shaking his head, Mr. Racjik reached for the loaf of bread in the center of the table, took two pieces, and dropped them into the toaster. "I guess I'd rather be against abortion and for the death penalty," he concluded, "than side with those who kill babies and coddle criminals."

Before Mrs. Racjik could say anything in response, her husband cleared his throat and nodded toward the door of the kitchen. Jill, their sixteen-year-old daughter, had just entered.

"Good morning, dear," her mother said sweetly. "I hope you slept well."

"Slept well? How could I sleep at all with the arguing going on out here?" she answered testily. "Come on! It's Saturday morning. People should be sleeping, not fighting."

"We were discussing, not fighting," Mr. Racjik corrected his daughter. "Besides, we don't need your permission to have a discussion."

"Maybe not, Dad," Jill said as she slipped into a chair by his side, "but the two of you need to think a little bit more before you have your next fight—I mean, discussion."

"Think? What do you mean, honey?" Mrs. Racjik was very curious to know what her daughter had in mind.

"Well, first, Dad says that killing murderers is okay, but killing cheerleaders isn't. Then you say that killing murderers isn't okay, but getting an abortion is. I just don't get it. If killing is wrong, it's wrong no matter who does it."

"How long were you standing outside the kitchen, Jill?" her father inquired. "Eavesdropping isn't polite, you know."

"I didn't have to eavesdrop. I could hear you in my bedroom," she huffed. "You two get so loud when you fight—I mean, discuss."

"She's right, Jim," Mrs. Racjik said. "It's no wonder she overheard us."

"Anyway, Mom and Dad," Jill said, covering a big yawn with her left hand, "I don't agree with either one of you. I think God loves all people, whether they're good or bad, and doesn't want anybody to be killed." She shook her head slightly. "Maybe you should pray today for a convict on death row, Dad, and Mom, you should pray for a pregnant teenager. I think everyone's life is worth at least a prayer or two, don't you?"

Seeing Your Own Story

- Why did Jill's parents get emotional when discussing the issues of abortion and capital punishment? Was Jill disrespectful of her parents in voicing her disagreement with their views?
- Whose position—Jill's, her mother's, or her father's—do you see reflected in the opinions of most of your friends? What is your position? Whose position do you think most clearly reflects the values of Jesus?

Seeing the Faith Story

The fifth commandment reminds us that God is the giver of all life. When we kill another human being, we take by violence what does not belong to us: a life designed and created by God. The Catholic church teaches that every human life is sacred from the womb to the tomb, and deserves full respect and protection under the law.

In the heated discussion of Jill's parents, we can see how difficult it is for us to be consistent in living out the fifth commandment. As Jill suggested, we need to pray for all those whose life is threatened and for all those who have taken the life of another. We need to pray for ourselves, too, that we may learn to respect human life in all its variety.

- If a friend of yours became pregnant and didn't know what to do, how would you act toward her? If a relative of yours were on death row, how would you act toward her or him?

You shall not murder. (Exodus 20:13)

Chris and Lee in Action

Chris's thoughts. This is great. Your parents won't be home for three hours, and we have the whole place to ourselves.

Lee's thoughts. We need some atmosphere here. I'll dim these lights and put on some music. I know. I'll even light some candles.

Chris's thoughts. Hmm. You're really trying to make this special, aren't you? I wonder: Are you thinking what I'm thinking?

Lee's thoughts. I love it when you smile at me like that. I wonder: Is something going to happen? I hope so.

Chris's thoughts. I think I'll get a little closer to you. I don't have to sit way over here, do I? Here I come. Hope I don't scare you off.

Lee's thoughts. This is easier than I thought it would be.

Chris's thoughts. This is easier than I thought it would be.

Lee's thoughts. There's that smile again. I think a kiss is coming. I know a kiss is coming. Here it comes.

Chris's thoughts. Hmm. This seems like the perfect time and place for a kiss.

Lee's thoughts. Hmm.

Chris's thoughts. Hmm.

Lee's thoughts. Now, I'm the one smiling.

Chris's thoughts. I can tell you liked that. Let me know if you like this.

Lee's thoughts. What are you doing?

Chris's thoughts. What's the matter—you're not getting shy on me now, are you?

Lee's thoughts. I didn't think you were going to unbutton my shirt. Did I ask you to do this? Is this what I want?

Chris's thoughts. Well, if you're going to stop me, let me know now. Come on, I'm looking right at you. Let me know if this is what you want.

Lee's thoughts. You're looking right at me. You're waiting for me to let you know whether this is okay. What do I do? What do I say? I never did this before. If I let you do this, where will it lead? What next? I'm not so sure about this. I just don't know.

Chris's thoughts. Come on now, don't leave me hanging here. My fingers are on the next button. One more button, and I'll know your decision. Come on, what will it be? What do you want? Send me a signal. Any time now. Okay, I waited. That must be a yes. Is it a yes? I think it's a yes. So here I come. Let me know if it's not a yes. Here I come. Let me know.

Seeing Your Own Story

- Obviously, Lee and Chris were not married. They were attracted to each other, and they were exploring their options. The story stopped before the evening ended. How do you think it should have ended? How do you think such evenings usually end in real life?

- Once two people become sexually involved, their relationship changes. If their sexual involvement ends, it is usually very difficult, if not impossible, for them to be friends. Why is this so? Have you observed this sort of awkwardness with any of your friends whose relationships have changed?

Seeing the Faith Story

God created us with sexuality. God created us with sexual feelings. God didn't create us this way so that we might take advantage of one another, or abuse one another, or use one another for selfish pleasure. God created us to be sexual so that we might enjoy one another's pleasure—but only in the ideal situation, which is a faithful, committed partnership.

When two people marry, they declare their intentions to create such a partnership. Their promises to be faithful partners are made to God and to the entire community that gathers on their wedding day to celebrate their love. The sixth commandment protects such promises by forbidding adultery (sex outside marriage). Many Christians believe that having sex before marriage, like adultery, is basically dishonest: the commitment implied by the sexual contact does not exist.

- Common sense supports what the church says about sexual activity outside marriage. Pregnancy, AIDS and other sexually transmitted diseases, and the emotional devastation of a breakup are some of the consequences that teenagers are likely to deal with if they choose to be sexually active. In your opinion, what are the most convincing reasons that unmarried teenagers should not become sexually active?

You shall not commit adultery. (Exodus 20:14)

More Money Than God

"Hi, Father Bill."

"Hi, Brandon. It's good to see you. How are you doing?"

"Not too bad, I guess, but I'm really nervous right now. I haven't been to confession in three years."

"Don't worry. I'll make it as easy as possible. What's on your mind?"

"Well, you see, Scott Teresio and I went to the mall yesterday just to hang out for a few hours. The stores were packed with people; I think everyone in town was Christmas shopping. When we walked into the Gap—you know, the clothing store?"

"Yes, I've heard of the Gap, Brandon."

"Just wanted to make sure, Father. Anyway, there were about six customers for every salesperson in the store, and . . . and . . ."

"Take your time, Brandon. There's no hurry."

"Well, Teresio told me to pick out a pair of jeans and try them on just for kicks. 'But I don't have any money,' I told him. 'What's the use?' 'Just pick out a pair, okay, Beyers?' he said, and so I did. He took a pair, too, and we walked to the fitting rooms together. When he followed me into the same room, I . . . I . . ."

"You're doing fine. Just take your time."

"But I'm so embarrassed, Father. How can a person be so stupid?"

"You're human, like the rest of us, Brandon. We all do stupid things once in a while."

"Well, anyway, Scott closed the door behind us and proceeded to take all the tags off the new pair of jeans he was holding. 'Hey, wait a minute,' I whispered. 'You can't do that.' 'I can't?' he laughed. 'Well, I just did!' Then he quickly took off his shoes and pants, put the tags on the old pair of jeans, slipped on the new ones, put his shoes back on, and carefully folded the old pair. 'My Christmas present to the Gap,' he said. Then he pointed to the pair he was wearing. 'And the Gap's Christmas present to me.' Gosh, Father, I was so nervous I thought I was going to throw up."

"I'd have been nervous, too, Brandon. It's a good sign to be nervous when something bad is happening."

"That's not the worst of it, Father. Then Scott grabbed the new pair I was holding and began to remove the tags. 'Take off your pants,' he whispered, and when I shook my head, he got mad. 'I'm not going to do this alone, Beyers,' he said, scowling at me. 'Take 'em off now.' So I did, and . . . and . . ."

"And?"

"And he put the tags on my old pants and folded them, while I put the new ones on. No one noticed a thing when we left the fitting rooms and Scott hid the old Levis at the bottom of a big pile of new Gap jeans. 'I think I'm sick,' I told him as soon as we were out the door. 'Don't get so worked up,' he laughed, slapping me on the back. 'The Gap has more money than God. This company could afford to give me twenty pairs!'"

"Scott has a persuasive tongue, doesn't he?"

"He could talk anyone into anything, Father!"

"Then why do you hang around with him, Brandon?"

"Well, once in third grade, he beat up a bully who was picking on me in the cafeteria. We've been pals ever since."

"You know, sometimes we outgrow our friendships, Brandon. Maybe you need to talk to him, and if he doesn't let you say what you're feeling without mocking you or making you feel stupid, you need to find another friend."

"Maybe I do."

"And you need to decide what you're going to do with the jeans you stole."

"Oh, I took care of that already, Father. As soon as Scott dropped me off at home, I got some money, hopped on my bike, raced to the mall, found my old pair of pants, went back to the fitting room and put them on, and then paid fifty dollars for the new pair. I really can't afford them, but my brother's only a size smaller than I am, and I got his name in the family draw, so I'll give him some new jeans for Christmas."

"You know, you're a fine young man, Brandon Beyers."

"I don't feel very fine, Father."

"That's because your conscience is still smarting. It wants you to remember this incident the next time someone tries to pull you away from your own values and common sense."

"But do you think God will forgive me?"

"Brandon, you can count on it. When you were returning to the mall to get your old pair of jeans, God was helping you pedal the bike."

Seeing Your Own Story

- Why did the priest tell Brandon that his nervous feeling about stealing the jeans was a good sign? Do you agree with the priest? Should Brandon have turned Scott in when he returned to the store to pay for the jeans?

- Do you believe that someone who records a friend's CD onto a cassette instead of buying her own CD is stealing? or that someone who copies words from a book and pretends that he wrote them is stealing? Why or why not?

Seeing the Faith Story

Taking something that belongs by right to another person or group of persons is a violation of the seventh commandment. It does not matter whether we take that something from a store or from a person. It also does not matter whether we steal a CD or tape, or make a copy of one that we do not own—both acts involve taking what does not belong to us. The bottom line is that people have a right to be secure in all their possessions.

Brandon realized that his friend's argument about stealing from a wealthy company was not convincing, yet he was not able to resist the pressure that his friend was exerting. As we grow into adulthood, life sometimes forces us into situations in which we must make unpopular decisions to remain true to our values. This may mean making the difficult choice to confront others when necessary.

- Would you be more likely to steal money if you knew you wouldn't get caught? Why or why not?
- How difficult is it for you to confront friends who are pressuring you to act contrary to your values?

You shall not steal. (Exodus 20:15)

Pushing the Limits of Honesty

Wednesday, 18 October

Dear Megan,

How's my favorite sister? I hope college is going well for you. I used to think my life in high school was boring, but today was anything but boring. In fact, I had more excitement than I ever want to see again!

Today I told a lie. But I think it was an important lie.

I was home alone. There was a lot of noise outside in the street.

Teenagers were shouting and running around. I could tell they were looking for someone. I got scared and locked the front door. Before I could get to the back door, I heard a noise in the kitchen. Someone had come into the house! It was a young boy! He was crying and begging me to let him hide. He was speaking broken English, and I could tell by his accent that his main language was Spanish. I told him, in my broken Spanish, to go downstairs. He ran. I locked the back door.

Before I could run upstairs to escape this madness, the teenagers on the street had come onto the front porch. They were pounding on the front door, all yelling at once: "Where is he? Is he in there? Are you hiding him? Let us in! Let us at him."

I yelled back at them through the locked door: "There's no one here. I don't know what you are talking about. I'm calling the police." And so I started to dial 911. But several police cars were arriving already. Someone else must have beaten me to it. The police took the screaming people away, and no one seemed to know that the scared little boy was hiding in our basement.

I called Dad right away. He came home immediately, went into the basement, calmed the boy down, and took him home. Dad said I did the right thing. . . .

» » » « « «

Wednesday, 18 October

Dear Bridgette,

How's my favorite sister? I hope high school is still fun for you. College is harder than I thought it would be, but more fun as well. Today was especially hard.

I broke a promise today. But it was an important promise to break.

My roommate has an eating disorder called anorexia bulimia. She's lost at least ten pounds since the semester began, and it was most obvious to me because I live with her. She hardly ever eats in public. When she eats in our room, she overeats, and then disappears into the bathroom. I confronted her on this two weeks ago, and she begged me not to say anything to anyone. She promised she would get help. So, I promised not to tell. I told her she could trust my word. But nothing has changed. She keeps doing her thing. Mostly not eating (that's the anorexia part) and occasionally bingeing and then vomiting (that's the bulimia part).

Her parents visited her today. After she ate six of her mother's homemade brownies, she went into the bathroom. She was there several minutes. Her parents asked me: "Does Laura look healthy to you? We are so worried about her." So, I told them the whole story. By the time she came back from the bathroom, we were all crying, and she knew I had told them.

Both Laura and her parents said I did the right thing. . . .

Seeing Your Own Story

• What do you think happened to the scared boy that Bridgette hid in the basement? Was everything okay for him once he got home? What kind of additional help or support might he have needed? Have you ever been in a situation like Bridgette's?

- What do you think happened to Laura next? Did she stop her dangerous eating behaviors, or did she continue them? What kind of additional help or support might she have needed? Have you ever been in a situation like Megan's?

Seeing the Faith Story

The eighth commandment is about telling the truth. Bridgette withheld the truth in order to help a person escape a violent situation. Megan broke a promise in order to help a suffering person escape an unhealthy situation. At first, it seems as if both girls could be accused of breaking the eighth commandment. But a deeper look shows that their situations are too complicated for a simple judgment.

In the first situation, the angry gang had no right to demand that Bridgette co-operate with them in violence. When they asked, "Is he in there?" they were really asking, "Will you help us hurt him?" Brigette's answer was an honest, "No, I will not co-operate with you in violence."

In the second situation, Megan agreed to keep Laura's secret only because Laura agreed to get help with her problem. Because Laura's health was at risk, and she apparently wasn't strong enough to get help on her own, Megan was not bound to keep that secret.

These situations are unusual. Typically when we lie, we are purposely keeping the truth from a person who has the right to know the truth. When we do that, we are being dishonest. And our dishonesty is wrong because good relationships can only be built on honesty and trust.

- Megan's and Bridgette's situations pushed the limits of honesty. But the sisters both did the right thing. They didn't tell a real lie or break a real promise. Yet every day, people tell real lies and break real promises. What does dishonesty do to a relationship? Has dishonesty ever hurt one of your close relationships? If so, how?

You shall not bear false witness against your neighbor. (Exodus 20:16)

Two Opposite Conversations

Inside a modest home, this conversation can be heard between two brothers:

"Dad won't let me get a motorcycle like Hal's."

"Dad won't let me get new basketball shoes like Rudy's. I'd love to have them. They're my size; maybe I could just walk off in them someday after practice."

"Dad won't let me get a new CD player like Judy's. I'd like to 'borrow it' sometime—know what I mean?"

"Yeah, and Dad won't let us have our own telephone. All my friends have their own telephone."

"Yeah. Dad won't let us have our own computer, either. All my friends have their own computer."

"Yeah, Dad won't let us have anything. I wish we had better stuff."

» » » « « «

Just a few miles away, this conversation can be heard between two homeless friends:

"Wow! Where did you find that sweatshirt? It looks almost new!"

"It was left on the bench by the bus stop. Do you want it? You can have it. My old one is in better shape than yours."

"Thanks! It's getting colder these days. We'd better start thinking about where to spend our nights. Last spring, the cops found our old winter hiding spot, so we can't go back there."

"Yeah, but we had that spot all winter. We were really lucky. It took them months to discover our secret! Don't worry. We'll find another spot. I've got a few ideas. How about food for tonight?"

"Hey, I brought you a hamburger. I found two in the dumpster behind the arcade. They weren't even touched. Someone probably ordered too much and couldn't finish. Today is our day!"

"Yep, that's a tough one to beat! We'll eat well tonight."

"And tomorrow, the weekly soup supper starts up again at Saint Bart's Catholic Church!"

"That's right! Two days in a row with great food! We really can't complain. God is good."

"Yes, indeed. God is good."

Seeing Your Own Story

- The brothers were so greedy that they didn't appreciate how fortunate they were. How do people become so envious of others?
- The homeless friends were so grateful for

56

what little they had that they were actually happy. How do people become so appreciative?

- Do you tend to be on the envious side or the grateful side? What do you think of your attitude? How could you improve it?

Seeing the Faith Story

What a contrast! The homeless friends had almost nothing to call their own, and yet they appreciated what they did have: "God is good."

And then there was the pair of brothers with a roof over their head, clothes on their back, and a father who cared about them, and yet they complained: "I wish we had better stuff."

The difference is attitude. That is what the ninth and tenth commandments are all about —not envying or coveting things or relationships. The brothers were covetous and ultimately unhappy. The homeless friends were not covetous, and though they had little, they were happy and thankful.

- How might a widespread attitude of envy affect the world? How might a widespread attitude of gratitude affect the world?
- Why is it sinful to be envious or covetous?

You shall not covet . . . (Exodus 20:17)

Appendix A: In Case You Want to Know More

Straight from the Heart and Other Stories is one of five books in a series based on the principal topics of the Catholic faith. You may have noticed the italicized phrase at the end of each story. This phrase, which may be familiar to you, points to the particular topic highlighted in the story.

The first story of this book, "Straight from the Heart," has a concluding sentence that reads, "Moses . . . said . . . : Hear, O Israel, the statutes and ordinances that I am addressing to you today." This sentence is from the Old Testament Book of Deuteronomy, chapter 5, verse 1. Here, Moses proclaims the Law of God to the Chosen People, beginning with the most famous list of law in human history: the Ten Commandments. The Ten Commandments are a kind of summary of the moral attitudes and principles that Jews and Christians live by.

Each story in this book is a mirror for understanding at least one of the Ten Commandments (the ninth and tenth commandments are combined in the final story). If you want to know more about how the Commandments are to be lived today, you can consult the following table. In this table, four sections appear for each story except the introductory story:

1. the commandment or commandments the story is connected to, as quoted in the Bible
2. a short summary of the concept emphasized in the story
3. a relevant citation from the *Catechism of the Catholic Church*
4. a notation of paragraphs from the *Catechism* that provide background on the commandment or commandments

"Straight from the Heart"
This story introduces the book and discusses the importance of laws and the Commandments.

"Taking a Cookie Break"
1. "I am the LORD your God . . . ; you shall have no other gods before me" (Exodus 20:2–3).
2. Hold God as number one.
3. "'When we say "God" we confess a constant, unchangeable being, always the same, faithful and just, without any evil'" (*Catechism*, number 2086).
4. *Catechism*, numbers 2084 to 2132

"Ice Cream, TV, and Baby-Sitting"
1. "You shall not make wrongful use of the name of the LORD your God" (Exodus 20:7).
2. Respect God's name.
3. "The second commandment forbids the abuse of God's name" *(Catechism,* number 2146).
4. *Catechism,* numbers 2142 to 2159

"The Guy in the Tie"
1. "Remember the sabbath day, and keep it holy" (Exodus 20:8).
2. Value sacred time and space.
3. "God entrusted the sabbath to Israel to keep as a sign of the irrevocable covenant" *(Catechism,* number 2171).
4. *Catechism,* numbers 2168 to 2188

"A Real Man"
1. "Honor your father and your mother" (Exodus 20:12).
2. Respect your parents.
3. "We should honor our parents to whom we owe life and who have handed on to us the knowledge of God" *(Catechism,* number 2197).
4. *Catechism,* numbers 2197 to 2246

"It's Wrong No Matter Who Does It"
1. "You shall not murder" (Exodus 20:13).
2. Hold all human life sacred.

3. "'Human life is sacred because from its beginning it involves the creative action of God and it remains for ever in a special relationship with the Creator, who is its sole end'" *(Catechism, number 2258).*
4. *Catechism,* numbers 2258 to 2317

"Chris and Lee in Action"
1. "You shall not commit adultery" (Exodus 20:14).
2. Be faithful in marriage.
3. "Sexuality affects all aspects of the human person" *(Catechism, number 2332).*
4. *Catechism,* numbers 2331 to 2391

"More Money Than God"
1. "You shall not steal" (Exodus 20:15).
2. Respect the possessions of others.
3. "Even if it does not contradict the provisions of civil law, any form of unjustly taking and keeping the property of others is against the seventh commandment" *(Catechism, number 2409).*
4. *Catechism,* numbers 2401 to 2449

"Pushing the Limits of Honesty"
1. "You shall not bear false witness against your neighbor" (Exodus 20:16).
2. Be truthful.
3. "Lying consists in saying what is false with the intention of deceiving the neighbor

who has the right to the truth" *(Catechism,* number 2508).

4. *Catechism,* numbers 2464 to 2503

"Two Opposite Conversations"

1. "You shall not covet . . ." (Exodus 20:17).
2. Be grateful and detached from possessions.
3. "Envy is a capital sin. It refers to the sadness at the sight of another's goods and the immoderate desire to acquire them for oneself, even unjustly" *(Catechism,* number 2539).
4. *Catechism,* numbers 2514 to 2527, and 2534 to 2550

Appendix B: Series Chart

The stories in the books of this series were written to reflect the structure of the *Catechism of the Catholic Church*. Each book corresponds to a major section of the *Catechism*, and the stories in it correspond to some—not all—of the articles in that section. The following chart gives an overview of this connection. This chart can help youth ministry leaders, teachers, and catechists identify stories that relate to a particular topic or topics.

That First Kiss and Other Stories

This book is connected to part 1, "The Profession of Faith," of the *Catechism*. The individual stories in it correspond to sections of the Apostles' Creed. The following table identifies the faith theme explored by each story:

Story Title	*Faith Theme*
"That First Kiss"	Introduction
"When You Care Enough to Give the Very Best"	Trinity
"The Best of Both Worlds"	Image of God

"So, Big Deal!"	Creation and stewardship
"Seeing Double"	Incarnation
"Waiting and Listening"	Mary, mother of God
"A New Way to Live and Die"	Salvation
"Back from the Dead"	Resurrection
"The Light at the End of the Tunnel"	Last judgment
"Enjoying the Differences"	Holy Spirit
"A Glorious Night for an Eclipse"	Church, people of God
"My Own Special Saints in Heaven"	Communion of saints
"A Little Bit of Heaven"	Eternity, heaven

My Wish List and Other Stories

This book is connected to part 2, "The Celebration of the Christian Mystery," of the *Catechism*. The individual stories in it correspond to the seven sacraments. The following table identifies the sacrament explored by each story:

Story Title	*Sacrament*
"My Wish List"	Introduction

"College Jitters"	Baptism
"All That Matters"	Confirmation
"In Memory of Jesus"	Eucharist
"Do We Need Gas?"	Reconciliation
"Seeing Stars"	Anointing of the sick
"The Best Vocation in the World"	Holy orders
"Why Get Married?"	Marriage

Better than Natural and Other Stories

This book is connected to part 3, "Life in Christ," of the *Catechism*. The individual stories in it correspond to the formation of conscience and to the human and theological virtues. The following table identifies the virtue explored by each story:

Story Title	*Virtue*
"Better than Natural"	Introduction
"To Cheat or Not to Cheat"	Conscience formation
"Pink Flowers Instead of Yellow"	Prudence
"People Who Are Not Like Us"	Justice

"This Is Unreal"	Fortitude (courage)
"The Big College Weekend"	Temperance
"Gee, Joy, I Don't Think So"	Faith
"Paints and Flowers"	Hope
"The Best Medicine"	Love (charity)

Straight from the Heart and Other Stories

This book is also connected to part 3, "Life in Christ," of the *Catechism*. The individual stories in it correspond to the Ten Commandments. The following table identifies the moral teaching explored by each story:

Story Title	*Moral Teaching*
"Straight from the Heart"	Introduction
"Taking a Cookie Break"	Hold God as number one.
"Ice Cream, TV, and Baby-Sitting"	Respect God's name.
"The Guy in the Tie"	Value sacred time and space.
"A Real Man"	Respect your parents.

67

"It's Wrong No Matter Who Does It"	Hold all human life sacred.
"Chris and Lee in Action"	Be faithful in marriage.
"More Money Than God"	Respect the possessions of others.
"Pushing the Limits of Honesty"	Be truthful.
"Two Opposite Conversations"	Be grateful and detached from possessions.

Meeting Frankenstein and Other Stories

This book is connected to part 4, "Christian Prayer," of the *Catechism*. The individual stories in it correspond to sections of the Lord's Prayer and to different types of prayer. The following table identifies the type of prayer explored by each story:

Story Title	Type of Prayer
"Meeting Frankenstein"	Introduction
"Oh, My God!"	Praise
"I Want to Tell You How Great I Think You Are"	Adoration and blessing
"Thank God!"	Thanksgiving

"Why Didn't You Answer My Prayers?"	Petition
"Playing with Fire"	Sorrow
"Asking for Too Much"	Intercession
"Sitting on Life's Park Bench"	Meditation
"Empty Your Head and Let God Fill It"	Contemplation

Acknowledgments *(continued)*

Titles in the Series

That First Kiss and Other Stories
My Wish List and Other Stories
Better than Natural and Other Stories
Straight from the Heart and Other Stories
Meeting Frankenstein and Other Stories

Order these titles from your local religious bookstore, or from us in one of these ways:

- Write to us at this address:
  Saint Mary's Press
  702 Terrace Heights
  Winona MN 55987-1320
- Call us at 800-533-8095.
- Look us up on the Internet at *www.smp.org*.